Drawing Is Fun!

DRAWING SPORTS FIGURES

Gareth Stevens
Publishing

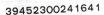

Please visit our Web site, www.garethstevens.com. For a free color catalog of all our high-quality books, call toll free 1-800-542-2595 or fax 1-877-542-2596.

Library of Congress Cataloging-in-Publication Data

Cook, Trevor, 1948-
Drawing sports figures / Trevor Cook and Lisa Miles.
    p. cm. — (Drawing is fun!)
Includes index.
ISBN 978-1-4339-5074-2 (pbk.)
ISBN 978-1-4339-5075-9 (6-pack)
ISBN 978-1-4339-5028-5 (library binding)
1. Sports in art—Juvenile literature. 2. Action in art—Juvenile literature. 3. Athletes in art—Juvenile literature. 4. Drawing—Technique—Juvenile literature. I. Miles, Lisa. II. Title.
NC825.S62C66 2011
743.4—dc22
                                2010027761

First Edition

Published in 2011 by
Gareth Stevens Publishing
111 East 14th Street, Suite 349
New York, NY 10003

Copyright © 2011 Arcturus Publishing

Artwork: Q2A India
Text: Trevor Cook and Lisa Miles
Editors: Fiona Tulloch and Joe Harris
Cover design: Akihiro Nakayama

Picture credits: All photographs supplied by Shutterstock; except pages 24, 28, and 30, supplied by iStockphoto; and page 26 supplied by photos.com.

Printed in the United States

CPSIA compliance information: Batch #AW11GS: For further information contact Gareth Stevens, New York, New York at 1-800-542-2595.

SL001765US

Contents

Gymnast

In gymnastics, people do special exercises.

The moves are hard. She makes them look easy.

She must practice every day.

She stands on one leg to do this exercise.

FUN FACTS ● FUN FACTS ● FUN FACTS ● FUN FACTS ● FUN FACTS

The first gymnasts lived in Greece more than two thousand years ago!

1. This shape is the body and the head.

2. One arm is reaching up.

3. She balances on her toes.

4. Her other leg is high behind her.

Ballet dancer

Ballet is a type of dance. The dancer makes it look beautiful.

The dancer needs strong arms and legs.

This ballet skirt is called a tutu.

She dances on the tips of her toes.

FUN FACTS ● FUN FACTS ● FUN FACTS ● FUN FACTS ● FUN FACTS

Dancers wear out ballet shoes very quickly. Some dancers get through two pairs each week!

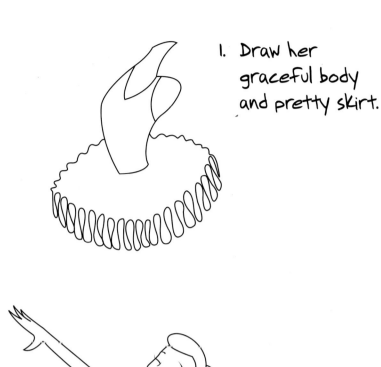

1. Draw her graceful body and pretty skirt.

2. Her hair is put up in a bun.

3. Her arms are held out wide to help her balance.

4. She balances tall on one leg.

Horse rider

The riding hat protects the rider if she falls.

She guides the horse using these reins.

The rider speaks to the horse.

She uses her feet to tell the horse to go fast or slow.

FUN FACTS ● FUN FACTS ● FUN FACTS ● FUN FACTS ● FUN FACTS

Horse riders sometimes play sports together. The winning horse and the rider may both get a medal!

1. Draw the horse's body and the rider's body.

2. Give the rider a hat. Start the horse's legs.

3. Now draw the other two legs.

4. Make the horse and the rider smile.

Skateboarder

Skateboards can go very fast!

A skater can do tricks. He makes the board jump into the air.

He wears skate shoes and baggy clothes. These clothes let him move easily.

The top of the skateboard is rough. It helps the skater stay on.

FUN FACTS ● FUN FACTS ● FUN FACTS ● FUN FACTS ● FUN FACTS

Skateboarding was started by surfers. They wanted something to do when there were no waves!

1. It's a head with a hat and a body.

2. Put in two strong legs.

3. Add his arms to help him balance.

4. Finish off with some pads on his elbows and knees.

Hang glider

A hang glider is like a huge kite. It has one big wing.

The wind lifts it into the air.

The person flying the hang glider is called the pilot.

He makes the hang glider take off. He runs then jumps into the air.

FUN FACTS ● FUN FACTS ● FUN FACTS ● FUN FACTS ● FUN FACTS

Pilots can fly in their hang gliders for hours. They can travel hundreds of miles!

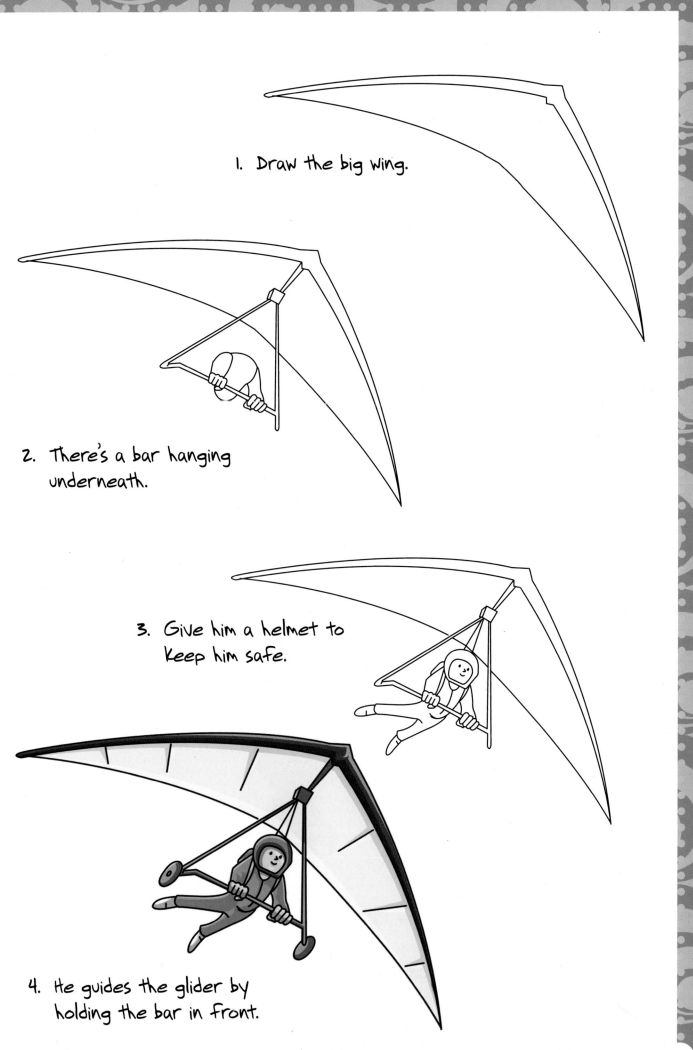

1. Draw the big wing.

2. There's a bar hanging underneath.

3. Give him a helmet to keep him safe.

4. He guides the glider by holding the bar in front.

Ice-skater

An ice-skater dances on ice.

The skater's arms and legs make pretty shapes.

She skates to music. She has to keep time.

Ice skates help the skater to spin and jump.

FUN FACTS ● FUN FACTS ● FUN FACTS ● FUN FACTS ● FUN FACTS

Some ice-skaters dance on ice. Others have races or play a game called ice hockey!

1. Draw her two arms first.

2. Now add her head with her hair put up.

3. She's skating on one leg.

4. Give her a short skirt with lots of folds.

Windsurfer

The wind blows the windsurfer across the water.

The sail traps the wind. It pushes the board along.

He has to know where the wind is coming from.

A windsurfer can do tricks. He can also take part in races.

FUN FACTS ● FUN FACTS ● FUN FACTS ● FUN FACTS ● FUN FACTS

Some people windsurf on indoor pools. Big fans make the wind!

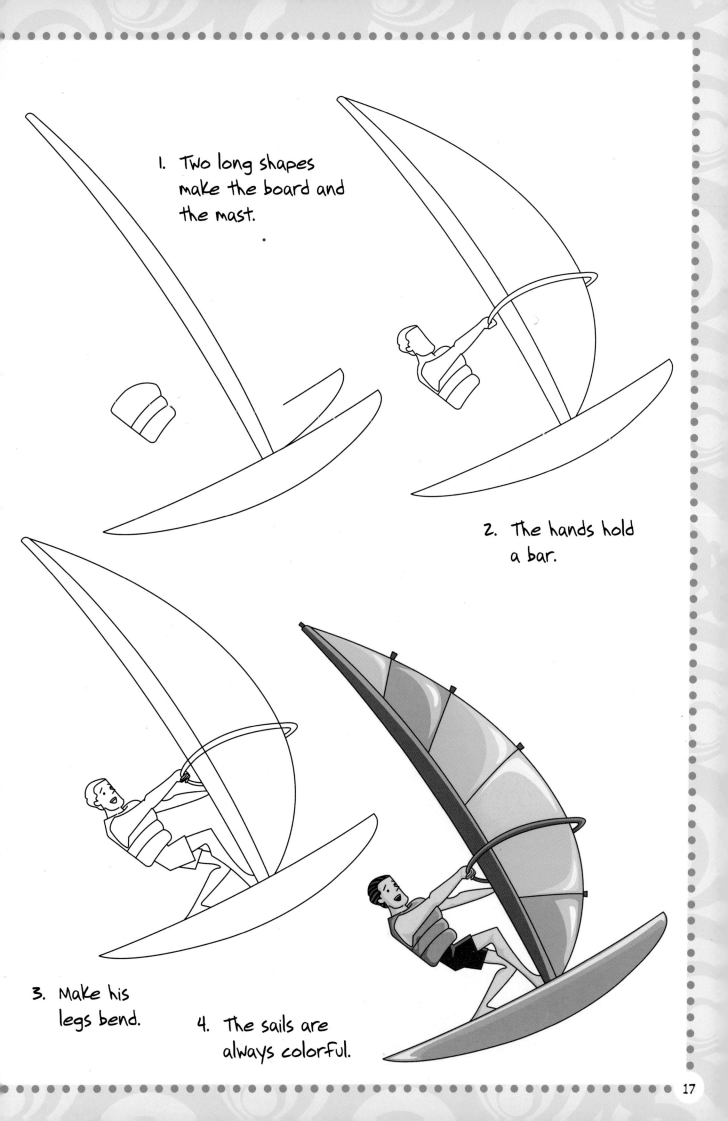

1. Two long shapes make the board and the mast.

2. The hands hold a bar.

3. Make his legs bend.

4. The sails are always colorful.

Roller skater

This skater wears a helmet on his head.

Some skates have two wheels at the front and two at the back.

He wears pads on his knees.

These are called inline skates. The wheels are in a line.

FUN FACTS ● FUN FACTS ● FUN FACTS ● FUN FACTS ● FUN FACTS

Roller skates were first used in a play. The play was in London, England, more than 250 years ago!

1. His body's quite thin.

2. He has long legs.

3. Draw his arms spread out for balance.

4. Give him elbow pads and a helmet in case he falls.

Tennis player

A tennis player hits the ball with a bat called a racket.

He can hit the ball soft or hard.

He hits the ball over a net.

Tennis shoes help him turn and run fast.

FUN FACTS ● FUN FACTS ● FUN FACTS ● FUN FACTS ● FUN FACTS

Some players hit the ball very hard. It travels twice as fast as a car on a highway!

1. Here's his body and head.

2. Now put in his arms and hands.

3. He's reaching up to serve the ball.

4. He dresses mostly in white.

Soccer player

A soccer player plays on a team. There are 11 people in his team.

He can't touch the ball with his hands or arms.

Each team has a color. The player wears it on his shirt and shorts.

Special soccer shoes help him to run and kick.

FUN FACTS ● FUN FACTS ● FUN FACTS ● FUN FACTS ● FUN FACTS

Soccer is the most popular ball game in the world.

1. Draw the body first.

2. Put on his head and arms.

3. He is running fast.

4. Don't forget the ball!

Baseball player

A baseball player wears a cap. It keeps the sun out of his eyes.

This player is a hitter. He holds a baseball bat.

His uniform shows the colors of his team.

The player who throws the ball is called the pitcher.

FUN FACTS ● FUN FACTS ● FUN FACTS ● FUN FACTS ● FUN FACTS

The longest baseball game ever lasted eight hours!

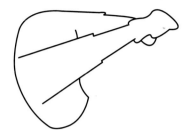

1. Draw his arms and the top of his body.

2. Add his head.

3. Put in his long legs.

4. He's just hit the ball!

Deep-sea diver

The diver wears these flippers on his feet. They help him swim fast.

He carries a tank on his back. The tank is full of air.

He can stay under the water for around an hour.

He wears a diving suit. It stops him from getting cold.

FUN FACTS ● FUN FACTS ● FUN FACTS ● FUN FACTS ● FUN FACTS

Some divers don't wear air tanks. They are called free divers. Free divers can hold their breath for a long time.

1. Draw the body and helmet.

2. Next put on the arms.

3. He's got gloves and flippers.

4. He has his own air in a tank on his back.

Boxer

A boxer has to be strong and quick.

He wears padded gloves. The gloves stop his hands from being hurt.

He wears baggy shorts so that he can move quickly and easily.

Boxing is a sport where two fighters hit each other.

FUN FACTS ● FUN FACTS ● FUN FACTS ● FUN FACTS ● FUN FACTS

Boxers fight other boxers that weigh the same.
A really huge boxer can't fight a tiny one!

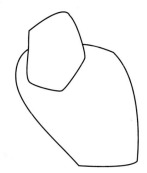

1. Two shapes make the head and the body.

2. He's punching with his right fist.

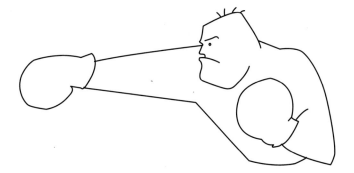

3. He's wearing big gloves.

4. He has a helmet to protect his head.

Flamenco dancer

Flamenco is a fast type of dance.

The dancer moves her arms. She claps her hands and stamps her feet.

She shows a lot of feeling when she dances. There is happiness and sadness in the song.

Her shoes make loud stomping sounds on the floor.

FUN FACTS ● FUN FACTS ● FUN FACTS ● FUN FACTS ● FUN FACTS

Sometimes the dancer makes up the steps as she dances. She doesn't practice them first!

1. Draw her head and graceful arms.

2. Add her skirt and face.

3. Give the skirt swirls.

4. A pretty red trim finishes her skirt.

Glossary

baggy hanging in a loose way

balance stand or move without falling over

bar a pole or rod

exercise moving in a way that makes you strong and fit

flipper a long, flat shoe that helps you to swim quickly

graceful a pretty way of moving

helmet a kind of hat you wear to stop you hurting your head

highway a fast road between cities

mast a pole that a sail is fixed to

pads these protect your elbows and knees if you fall

pilot someone who guides a plane or hang glider

protect stop someone from getting hurt

racket a type of bat with a long handle. It has a round part at the end with strings across it.

reins a rider holds these and uses them to guide a horse

rough not smooth

surfer someone who stands on a board and rides waves at the beach

tank something that is filled with a liquid, such as water, or a gas, such as air

tutu a skirt with lots of folds. Ballet dancers wear these.

Index

Further Reading

Halpern, Monica. *Explore and Draw Extreme Sports*. Rourke Publishing, 2010.

Soloff Levy, Barbara. *How to Draw Sports*. Dover Publications, 2009.

Tallarico, Tony. *Drawing and Cartooning All-Star Sports*. Perigree Trade, 1998.